OFF THE WALL
The World of WearableArt

Photography by Martin de Ruyter, Neil Price,
Rohit Chawla and Daniel Rose

WORLD OF WEARABLEART

craig potton publishing

Designers and Garments

The Purpose Kolia Co, New Zealand
Silk & polyester-cotton chiffon, spandex, nylon netting, fibreglass rods

Preface

WORLD OF WEARABLEART

In 1987, Nelson sculptor Suzie Moncrieff came up with an original idea to promote her rural art gallery. She decided to take the art off the wall, put it on the human body and design a theatrical show to present the creations. So was born the World of WearableArt™ Awards Show, or WOW® as it is now known in New Zealand.

Suzie encouraged a handful of Nelson designers to create garments for an audience of 200 people, unaware that this small beginning would evolve into a unique international phenomenon.

WOW® now attracts a remarkable range of international artists, designers, costume makers and craftspeople who work painstakingly and passionately to present their creations on stage in front of an annual audience of 50,000.

WOW® is best described as a glorious rebellion against the mundane, a choreographed collision where fantasy meets reality and dreams merge with nightmares. For the audience, it is sensory saturation, with the bodies on stage forming a moving canvas in a seamless, fluid exhibition that is enhanced by soundscapes, lighting, dance, drama and comedy. There is no narration, nor are there any language barriers.

WOW® is the most successful event of its type in the world. Judging is a highly competitive and selective process that sees both New Zealand and international entries whittled down to around a couple of hundred that will make it on stage. This exposure has launched, and often re-launched, the careers of many designers.

Over the years countless talented, dedicated and creative people have helped write the WOW® story. This includes the designers, the models and performers, the artistic and production teams, the sponsors, the audiences and the management team. Without their consistent passion and tireless commitment, Suzie's concept could never have flourished. This book is dedicated to all these people.

Owned and operated by World of WearableArt™ Limited, New Zealand is proud to host this international event, now in its third decade, and to keep it firmly grounded on local territory. The annual Awards show is staged in Wellington, while garments from the historic collection are on display all year round at the World of WearableArt™ & Classic Cars Museum in Nelson.

On stage, 2009 – Avant Garde Section, with **Lady Of The Wood**

Introduction

So much of who we are and where we're from is presented in what we wear and how we wear it. Since the beginnings of human history our bodies and what we put on them has formed a central pillar of cultural tradition. We've painted and tattooed them, and dressed them with ceremony and ritual to represent spiritual, social and sexual messages, usually as an expression of tribal cohesion and identity. Today, Western society's preoccupation with covering the body is dominated by the global fashion industry. It is a myopic focus however, that, irrespective of the skill and creativity of the design, encourages conformity and a preoccupation with branding. For most of us, the clothes we wear must fit with what is fashionable, while being safe, flattering, comfortable and usually not too outrageous.

For me, the joy and energy of WearableArt™ is that it enables designers to step out from these constraints, and to see the body as a blank canvas on which they can develop any idea that appeals to them. The more provocative, unorthodox and original, the better. The garments do not have to be commercially viable. They do not even have to take themselves seriously. The only thing they must be is wearable. Creators have the freedom to use painting, sculpture, textiles, costuming, engineering and electronics – in fact any medium to realise their vision, from 20,664 plastic collar stays to 600,000 glass beads, from human hair to wood, corrugated iron to kitchen utensils or taxidermied birds to sumptuous silks.

Too often, contemporary art is inaccessible and intimidating. WOW® is neither. The artists and designers are an eclectic mix, like their creations. They come from all walks of life and many different backgrounds, and there are few barriers to becoming involved. Creating a WearableArt™ garment doesn't have to be an expensive process, and it encourages lateral and original thinking. It is also about being inventive with recycled materials or creating materials from scratch.

I regularly competed in competitions as an artist so I appreciate the hours of painstaking work that go into creating an art piece. I know also, the vulnerability of presenting yourself and your work to judges, and the fear of exposing yourself, via your work. Rejection is brutal in any context. So I respect the strength, resilience and tenacity that this demanding experience requires, especially when artists don't make it. It takes conviction, determination and self-belief to keep

Persephone's Descent Stuart Johnson, New Zealand
Handmade components of mild and stainless steel, brass, chain

designing and creating, but the experience is often a rich one, both personally and professionally.

Even after 25 years of judging thousands of garments, I never tire of seeing the extent of creativity that WOW® generates, and it propels and inspires me to create yet another show. I urge the audiences never to take for granted the patience, the passion and the hours of dedication each individual work of art takes. It is truly inspiring and they, the artists, are truly inspirational.

Suzie Moncrieff

Ornitho-Maia Nadine Jaggi, New Zealand *Leather - wet moulded, embossed, carved, hand dyed, copper foiled & hand sewn; bronze buckles, steel rings*

American Dream Sarah Thomas, New Zealand *Vinyl, leather, papier mâché, builders' foam, plastic*

Rosa (Le Freak, C'est Chic) Gillian Saunders, New Zealand *Baling twine, tin, velvet*

Behind Closed Doors Kathryn Preston, Angie Robinson, New Zealand *1900 Formica samples, fishing line, glue*

'I was inspired by the texture, durability, and form of Formica, a product on many kitchen benches, used everyday by women. 1900 individual pieces of Formica were glued together, forming 100 pivoting strips linked by fishing line. The spreading out of this fan enables the discovery of a hidden, vibrant and beautiful personality, often kept away from view by the demands of appearing organized and happy as the perfect mother and wife. Women often feel frustrated and undervalued in that role yet deep down know that there is little more important that they could do.'

Tidal Traveller Rita Schrieken,
New Zealand *Driftwood, pumice,
shell, muka, fabric, papier mâché*

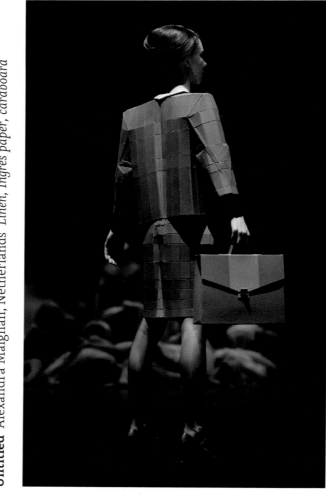

Untitled Alexandra Maignan, Netherlands *Linen, Ingres paper, cardboard*

'**Untitled** is built like a book cover, and incorporates the techniques of bookbinding. As a book cover, this costume can be seen as a shell, as armour, as social cover. It appears as a conventional suit, a trendy and timeless uniform, but I'm interested in what might be hiding underneath.'

Nothing But The Truth Thera Hillenaar, Netherlands
Stretch cotton, styrofoam balls

Lady La La Dinah Walker, Mark Walker, New Zealand *Fibreglass, wire, velvet, electronics, patent leather*

Clan Pacifica Janet Bathgate, New Zealand *Hand-cut closed cell foam, computer-designed digitally-printed fabrics, handcrafted printmaking techniques*

'**Clan Pacifica** was inspired by visiting The Scots in New Zealand exhibition at Te Papa; a story of Scottish inter-marriage with Maori; and a story of contributions to New Zealand – education, courage, determination, whiskey and the Woman's Christian Temperance Union! Clan Pacifica are the New Zealand-born Scottish people, some of mixed bloodlines – people who belong to this southern land by birth and spiritual connection, now established over a period of five generations.'

Alpha Romeo Tango Artpholstery
Wendy Burton, Sylvia Campbell,
New Zealand *Prints from Past
Pleasures, upholstery fabric, piping,
plastic*

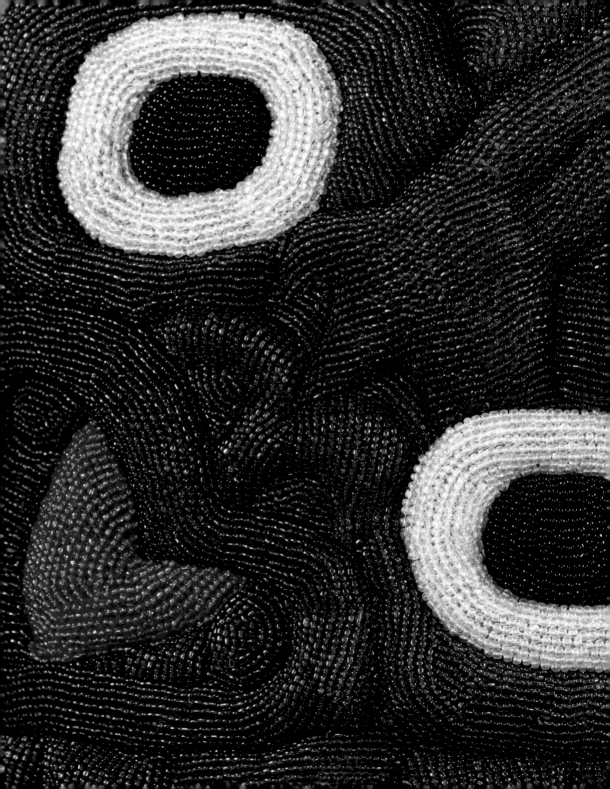

Tiki Touring Judith Keith, New Zealand
Fabric, 60,000 glass beads individually sewn and knotted

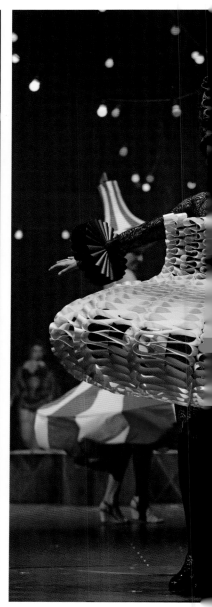

Zazel Kathryn Preston, Angie Robinson, New Zealand
Polypropylene cage, ribboning

LEFT **Fantale** Christine Heaney, New Zealand Curtains, cardboard, sticks, camping mat, plastic

MIDDLE **Belljar** Alice Eaton, New Zealand Tulle, plastic, paper, cotton

RIGHT **Spiralling Step** Emily Pierdinock-Hagen, United States Cotton broadcloth, paint, *stretch knit, wooden skewers*

Te Po (The Night) Shona Tawhiao, New Zealand *Harakeke, lining, wire, spray paint*

BioLumina Svenja, Australia *Organza, tulle, tubing, paint, elwire*

45

Madame Mathews As Marksheet Monster Ankur Kaushik, India *Polypropylene*

The Ring Mistress Richelle Dynae Rudeen, United Kingdom
Latex, wire, steel, satin

Budgerigar Brassiere Emily Valentine Bullock, Australia
Taxidermied budgerigars, feathers, rubber, fabric

Persephone's Descent   Stuart Johnson, New Zealand
Handmade components of mild and stainless steel, brass, chain

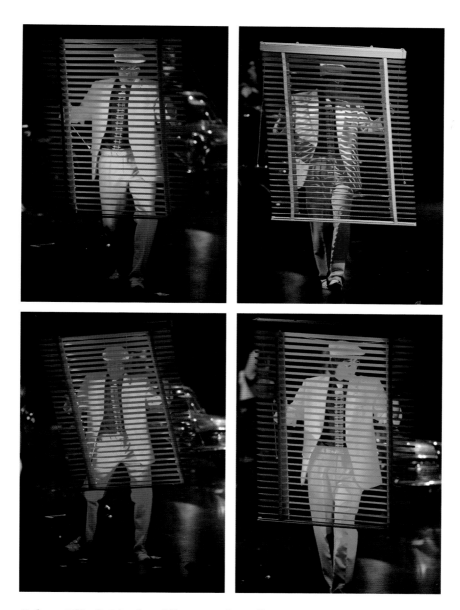

Colour Blind Dinah Walker, Mark Walker, New Zealand
Venetian blind, electronics, fabrics, metals

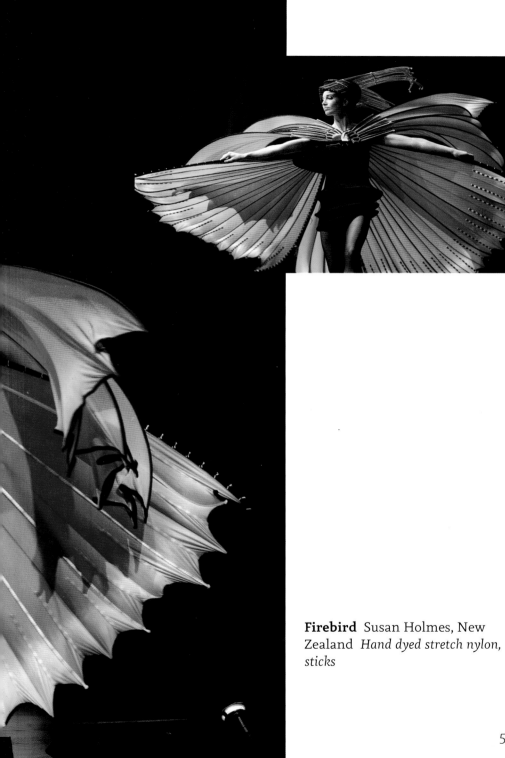

Firebird Susan Holmes, New Zealand *Hand dyed stretch nylon, sticks*

Multi-Plug Ragini Ahuja, Rishabh Rhode, India *Charger pins, bubble wrap, fabric*

Lagarus Ovatus En Masse Catherine Anderton, New Zealand
Grass, foam, faux fur, fibreglass, wire, fimo

'**Lagarus ovatus** is an exotic species of grass commonly known as Hare's-tail, and also often referred to as bunny or cotton tails. I love the beauty of this plant and I'm intrigued by how flora and fauna share similar characteristics. What would Darwin say?'

Poly-Prop Rosy Harray, New Zealand *400 metres fabric strips, steel, paint*

Cockroach Bra Pooja Rajput, India *Leather, wire, fabric*

Hands Off Mark Crocker, New Zealand *Kitchen utensils, nuts, bolts, bicycle inner tubes*

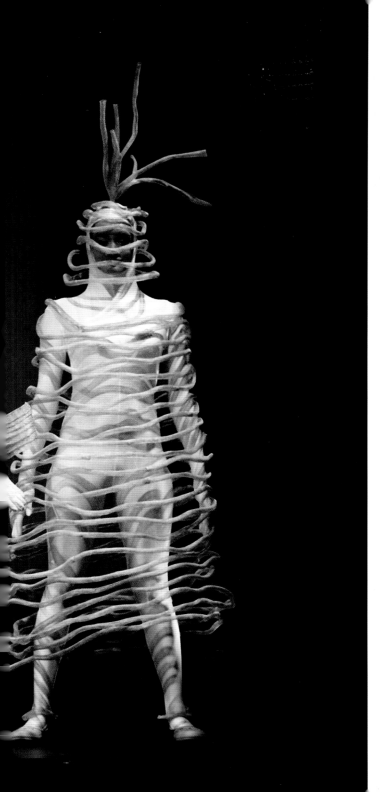

Screen Play Amy Jean Boebel, Sue Hobby, United States *Aluminium screen, monofilament*

Hei Tiki – The Director's Cut Sharon Flanagan, New Zealand *Celluloid film, stainless steel, Sellotape, cotton thread, nylon thread, flax cord*

'While born with his past in front of him, this model walks naked into his past, with a **Hei Tiki** made of film, holding his whakapapa or stories. Periodically he crouches and leans forward, allowing light to penetrate the symbol.'

Atomic Cactus Patch Sean Purucker, United States
Foam, hand sanded and hand painted earplugs, beads, fabric, plastic

Ultra Violent Beauty Nicola Richardson, Marianne Taviner, United Kingdom *Fabric, PVC, carbon fibre rod, nylon rod*

Flora Jeff Thomson, New Zealand *Corrugated iron*

Cumulus Sharon Reid, New Zealand *1400 plastic milk bottles, fabric, beads*

Bowled A Maiden Over Donna Allfrey, New Zealand *Recycled cricket pads, curtains, beads, paint*

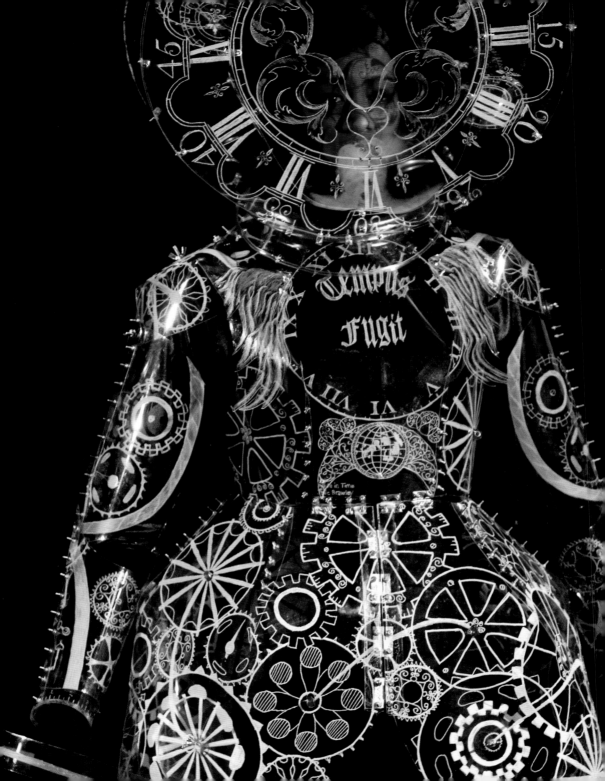

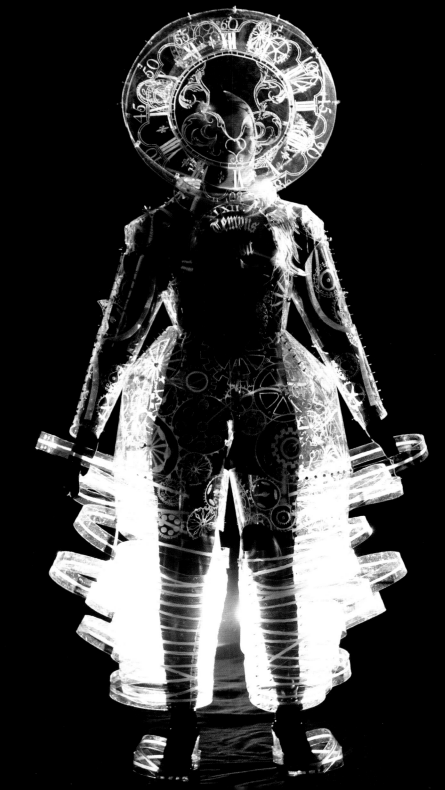

Reflection On Time Julie Brawley, New Zealand *Engraved Suntuff roofing, nuts, bolts*

Epona Rachael Galuszewski, New Zealand *Horsehair, saddlery, fabric*

Lady Of The Wood David Walker, United States
Mahogany, lacewood, maple, cedar

'My goal with this garment was to see how close I could get to reproducing a 17th Century ball gown made entirely out of wood. The lacewood bodice was made from a modified 17th Century pattern, while the mahogany sleeves were steam bent into shape and finished with a lacewood cuff. The skirt is an oval pannier with two cedar hoops supported from a mahogany belt covered with 52 stripped mahogany and maple veneer strips.'

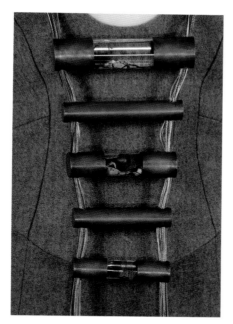

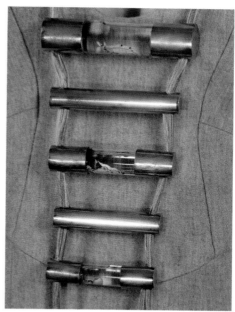

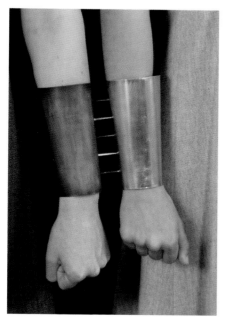

Bound Gina Digirolamo, Lindsey Eisentraut, United States
Wool, glass, copper, nickel, enamel, steel

On stage, 2010 – Avant Garde Section

Second Skin Hayley May, Fiona Christie, New Zealand
Lycra, tulle, nylon, sheepskin

Saddle Up Mary Wing To, United Kingdom *Leather hide, patent leather, natural silk, human hair. Each leather piece is hand cut, stained, moulded, laced and hand stitched to finish*

'No animal has inspired the creative instincts of man as much as the horse. The horse has shared man's triumphs, failures, hopes and frustrations since pre-historic times. This wild and spirited creature was known to have such power and mystique that it was dignified as a cult figure.'

Tubular Belle Ann Skelly, New Zealand *File folders, paper fasteners, cotton, net, clear floor matting, draught excluder, scrum helmet, wire, plastic tubing, velcro, brass eyelets, rings*

The Urchin Rita Schrieken, New Zealand *Driftwood, pumice, mutton cloth, papier mâché*

Lady Curiosity Fifi Colston, New Zealand *EVA foam, laminate, paint, velvet, acrylic mirrors*

'Tattooed ladies were a popular circus attraction of the late 19th Century; a peep show within a freak show. But it was not only performers who took to the art; ladies of society indulged too. When I read New Zealand author Rachael King's novel *Magpie Hall* I was inspired by her Victorian gothic elements of tattoos, taxidermied collections and a possible flayed woman. A Cabinet of Curiosities and its odd contents was something the fated Dora in the book had to contend with. Ultimately it was to be her downfall, her Memento mori.'

Seamless Octopus
Kim Kui Tang, Hong Kong
Hand looped iron wire

Dance Of The Calligrapher's Brush Judith Clemett, New Zealand
Styrene foamboard, fabric

'I was inspired by Asian brush calligraphy, both its precision, grace, stark colour scheme, and its mastery of simple form. I also admire the way this literary art can simultaneously become visual art. Many of these qualities can be seen in other Asian artistic disciplines, especially haiku poetry, and the haiku philosophy of strengthening an image by cutting to its essence is reflected in this garment.'

Horridus Lynn Christiansen, United States *Copper, silver and gold plating*

'Cutting, hammering, shaping... the physical involvement in working in metal is intoxicating. I've used metal to make jewellery and other wearable pieces, but I have never dressed the whole body. I wanted to challenge myself to create an outfit entirely out of metal that evokes a sense of power, protection and beauty. I began with my fascination with the Horny Devil lizard. I developed my ideas in sketches and models, but the metal dictates how a piece will evolve. I was delighted when the metal and I began to understand one another and the work came alive.'

On stage, 2010 – Children's Section

Queen Adelaide Emma Whiteside, New Zealand *Automotive radiator copper, fabric, aluminium*

'Queen Adelaide was a British Queen from 1830 to 1849, who had her personal jewels inlaid into a crown for her coronation in a bid to minimise 'unnecessary expenditure'. Even in death Adelaide wished to be buried 'free from the vanities of pomp and state'. She would have appreciated a dress made of recycled copper off-cuts, from the back streets of an Auckland industrial block.'

EOS Claire Prebble, New Zealand *Sterling silver wire, copper wire, glass beads, dupion, organza silk*

Tikini Gillian Saunders, New Zealand
Recycled baling twine, picture hooks, curtain rings

'It took hours untangling the massive bag of baling twine in the shed (which I'd brought back from my brother-in-law's farm years ago) and removing all traces of mouse, mud and straw (my cat was most useful during this process). After hours and hours of sewing plaits together, a stuffed shoulder and my neck put 'out' from having to sew using pliers, and piles of broken needles later, **Tikini** appeared.'

Put A Cork In It Sean Purucker, United States *Cork, resin, fabric, plastic, foam, glass*

Breathing Ru Xiang, Tang Wenjie, China *Fabric, acrylic, rubber tube*

The Love Of Icarus Rodney Leong, New Zealand
20,664 plastic collar stays, lycra

You Don't Bring Me Flowers Catherine Anderton, New Zealand *Velvet, leather, paint, ink*

'A discarded bunch of roses, once so beautiful and full of hope, has been left ignored too long in the vase. The romance seems over and the man of her dreams has turned out to be human. Our heroine walks through life full of false expectation and fulfilled disappointment. Bound, she can not leave, but nonetheless, for this poor girl, there's always hope.'

Who's The Pest... I Am The Pest!!! Beatrice Carlson,
New Zealand *Perspex, lycra, silk, feathers*

Something Wicked This Way Comes Eve Gilliland,
New Zealand *Brass, steel, bronze, leather, crystal*

Aurora Australis Sharon Reid, New Zealand
550 metres plastic corded strapping, acrylic drops and beads, fabric

Hidden Assassin Lauren Kidd, New Zealand *Possum skin, latex, fabric*

My Transfinite Memory Ankita Choudhury, Deepit Chugh, India
Aluminium, styrofoam, wool

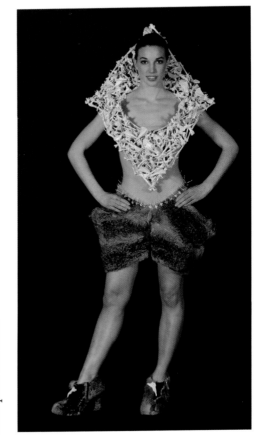

Just Hare-Say Keryn Whitney, New Zealand
Hare pelts and bones

'In the early 90's the British artist Damien Hirst began showing carcases of sheep, cattle and sharks whole and sliced in formaldehyde-filled glass and steel tanks. Many people found the resulting works to be confrontational and upsetting. They failed to 'see' the beauty of Mother Nature in the shapes, forms and patterns of the internal bones and soft tissue. I have long been fascinated with the strength, yet beauty of bones such as the scapula, coccyx and scull. Without being confrontational I have endeavoured to show that the amazing beauty of Mother Nature is not only surface deep.'

Loops Yogesh Chaudhary, Manas Barve, India
Merino wool felt

'**Loops** originates from the revolutionary technique of seamless knitting, and uses a laser-cut pattern which allows each panel to interlace with the others to form an interesting surface texture. Our concept with this garment was to achieve a self-sufficient independence without any interference from foreign substances, such as thread or glue.'

Rattle Your Dags Ursula Dixon, Paula Coulthard, New Zealand
Recycled wool fadges, wool, cycle helmet, merino horns, hemp rope, crystals

Into Thin Air Marie Gant Roxburgh, Christchurch
Foam board, dowel, photocopied photos, MDF

The Valkyrie War Maiden Melody Brook,
New Zealand *Used tea bags (thousands)
that were dried, sliced and the tea removed,
crocheted doilies, cardboard, buttons*

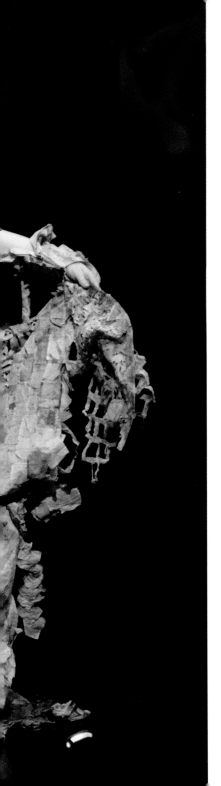

Funky Fungi Sean Purucker, United States
Foam, plastic, fabric, paint

Gondwana Susan Holmes, New Zealand
Hand dyed silk, panama straw

'When Australian artisan India Flint sent me this hand-dyed organza saying 'It's the best I've ever made' I was most reluctant to use it. It wasn't showy or graphic and it was brown (I never use brown!). But gradually, as I handled it, let the light shine through it and draped it, I fell in love with it and **Gondwana** evolved. The hat was needed to add to the arching line of the back. It's made from exquisite handwoven panama straw and has connotations of dry bones, parts of insects, pods, the medieval cap and protection from the blinding sunlight. **Gondwana** portrays the dry, haunting Australian landscape.'

Sir Lazyboy Cassandra Thomson, New Zealand *Vinyl, dome nails, foam, material*

Le Tatau (Tattoo) Lindah Lepou, New Zealand
Fabric, sequins, beads

Mana Uha Olivia Hall, New Zealand *Plastic strapping*

On stage, 2010 – Open Section

Homage To Black; Thinking Thin Mary Donald, New Zealand *Wooden skewers, hessian, satin, beading*

Bat Gear Vivan Sundaram, Pratima Pandey, India *Tyre tubes*

Rock On In The Shadowlands Janet Bathgate, New Zealand
Satin, painted interfacing

'My challenge was to create a distinctly New Zealand /
Asia-Pacific piece, yet exclude the familiar Maori motifs of
koru, kowhaiwhai, kotututuku, taniko. So I studied the first
art of New Zealand – the rock art of Te Wahipounamu,
including the drawn records of Tony Fomison and Theo
Schoon. Gradually I realised the essence of rock art is anima,
contained within. It is the patterning of this life force that I
am trying to convey, creating new shapes that echo the old,
reinterpreting forms from the cave shadows and bringing
them out into today's light.'

RIGHT **Psychedelic Symphony** Janice Elliott, New Zealand *Polystyrene, MDF, fabric*
FAR RIGHT **Wanderer** Sue Cederman, New Zealand *Cotton, nylon, paint, netting, wire, pape*

Let Me Bee Anmol Sharma, Siddharth Aredath,
India *String, wire, closed cell foam, hand stitched ribbon*

AM I I AM Rodney Leong, New Zealand
Acrylic sheeting, pleated polyester

Crystal Candela Bra Violet Oliver, New Zealand
Fabric, plastic

My Bra My Salvador Wendy Burton, New Zealand
Fabric moulded and hardened with fibreglass, rubber, acrylic paint

Raitzeilea Glenys Mann, Australia *Rooster and pheasant feathers, beads*

Ma'resauro Simon Hames, New Zealand *Mussel shells, fencing wire, velvet, saucepan*

Hat Couture Susan Holmes, New Zealand *Recycled hats (wool and straw), dyed hat straw, straw table mats*

'I inherited a pile of hats from a friend who had retired and was most inspired by the lightness and shape and dye-ability of the straw and wool. I have always loved the restrained simplicity of high fashion, but never dared to be in thrall of it before now in my wearable art. I kept trying to make my garment more complex, to be more clever and impressive, but it wouldn't let me, so here it is in all its simplicity!'

LEFT **This Is Not A Booby** Jo Torr, New Zealand
Cotton, feathers, foam rubber

RIGHT **Feathered Fetish** William Griffith, New Zealand
Sterling silver, labradorite stone and bird wings

Groper Julian Dirks, New Zealand
Polyester fibreglass, canvas strapping, rivets, paint,
1/2 gallon Mac's Gold and 1 gallon patience

The Burning Giraffe Pia Fischer, Germany *Textiles, plastic, wood*

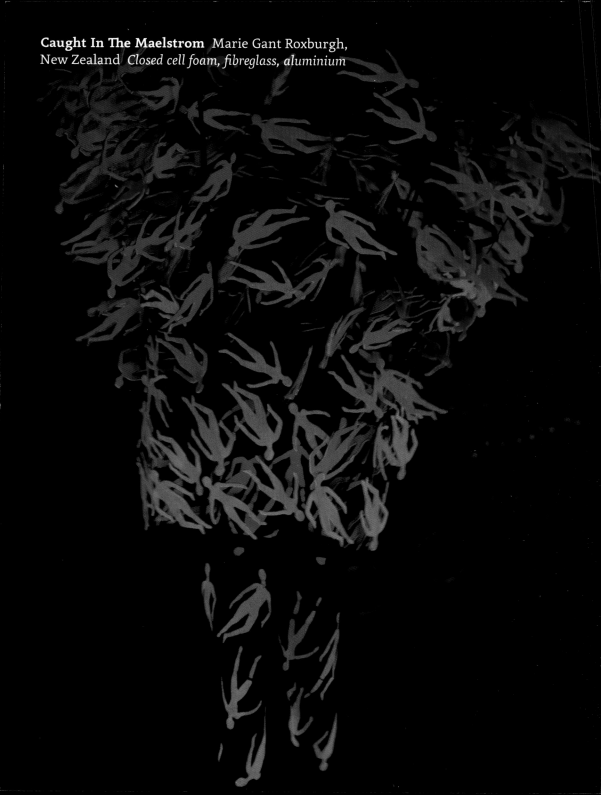

Caught In The Maelstrom Marie Gant Roxburgh,
New Zealand *Closed cell foam, fibreglass, aluminium*

Persephone In Cuba St. Fifi Colston, New Zealand
EVA foam, fabric, table tennis balls, hose pipe, boning

Let Them Drink Tea Angela Bright, Canada *Recycled tea bags, china, paper, coffee filters*

Afternoon Tea Horiana Reedy, Thelma Field, Cathie Williamson, New Zealand *Plywood, fabrics, icing, wire mesh*

Ecdysis Bonnie Begg, Christine White, Australia
Fabric, irrigation tubing, wire, foil

First published in 2011 by Craig Potton Publishing and the World of WearableArt™ Ltd

© Craig Potton Publishing and the World of WearableArt™ Ltd
www.craigpotton.co.nz
www.worldofwearableart.com

ISBN: 978-1-877517-42-6

Design by Robbie Burton
Photographs by Martin de Ruyter, Neil Price, Rohit Chawla, Daniel Rose

Printed in China by Midas Printing Co. Ltd

Front Cover: **You Don't Bring Me Flowers**/Catherine Anderton
Back Cover: **My Transfinite Memory**/Ankita Choudhury, Deepit Chugh

412102